# Praying the Rosary

## with Benedict XVI

by

Fr Donncha Ó hAodha

*All booklets are published thanks to the generous support of the members of the Catholic Truth Society*

CATHOLIC TRUTH SOCIETY

PUBLISHERS TO THE HOLY SEE

# Contents





*ISBN 978 1 78469 003 8*

# Introduction

## The Rosary as contemplation of Christ

St Luke is often regarded as the 'painter' of Our Lady. His Gospel *tableaux* of the person and vocation of the Mother of God are an inexhaustible source of meditation.[1] But the evangelist does not stop at an external depiction of Mary. Twice in the second chapter of his Gospel he gives a precious glimpse of the Blessed Virgin's soul: "Mary kept all these things, pondering them in her heart" (*Lk* 2:19; cf. v. 51). Our Lady is a contemplative whose loving gaze is constantly directed to her divine Son.[2] How often during the thirty-three years of Christ's earthly life his Mother's gaze must have lingered watchfully on the Incarnate Word (cf. *Jn* 1:14), the Emmanuel, God-with-us (cf. *Is* 7:14, *Mt* 1:23), the blessed fruit of her womb (cf. *Lk* 1:42).

The Holy Rosary, as St John Paul II beautifully explained in his 2002 Apostolic Letter, *Rosarium Virginis Mariae*,[3] is a participation in Mary's contemplation of the face of Jesus.[4] "To recite the Rosary is nothing other than to *contemplate with Mary the face of Christ*."[5] Indeed, in praying the Rosary, "the Christian community enters into contact with the memories and contemplative gaze of Mary".[6] The Rosary is "*an exquisitely contemplative prayer*"[7] the holy Pontiff explained, because it involves looking on Christ "at the school of Mary".[8] Moreover, to contemplate him through the eyes of the one who was most intimately united to Jesus and his will (cf. *Lk* 11:28) is to take the most direct route to "the depths of the Heart of Christ, ocean of joy and light, of suffering and of glory".[9]

Thus the Rosary is an essentially Christocentric prayer. Its "clearly Christological orientation"[10] is assured by its Marian perspective. In other words, to look on the central mysteries of salvation through the eyes and heart of the Saviour's Mother is to give oneself over to love of and "unceasing praise of Christ".[11] St John Paul II underlines the nature of the Rosary as "a form of Christocentric contemplation".[12] In this prayer, the faithful gaze on the face of Christ,[13] the One "in whom all the fullness of God was pleased to dwell" (*Col* 1:19), and who reveals the Father with whom he is one (cf. *Jn* 14:9-11).

To pray the Rosary is to be transformed by Christ, according to Christ, and unto Christ, in the progressive identification with the Lord Jesus in which holiness consists.[14] As Pope Francis explained on 1st May 2013, the Rosary leads us "to reflect on the key moments of Christ's life, so that, as with Mary and Joseph, he is the centre of our thoughts, of our attention and our actions".[15]

## The Rosary as a school of prayer

In the second joyful mystery we contemplate the Visitation of the Blessed Virgin to her kinswoman Elizabeth. The older lady hails "the mother of [her] Lord" (*Lk* 1:43), while her unborn child, St John the Baptist, rejoices in the presence of the Redeemer (cf. v. 44), and from the womb begins his ministry of announcing the Messiah. Then Mary's joy erupts in the *Magnificat* (cf. *Lk* 1:46-54). This sublime canticle refers to the past by echoing the hopes for salvation that Israel, and indeed all humanity, had cherished from the very beginning (cf. vv. 54-55). It refers to the present as an expression of Mary's gratitude and praise (cf. vv. 47-50) on being clothed with the sun (cf. *Rv* 12:1), by having conceived the "Sun of Justice" (cf. *Ml* 4:2). The *Magnificat* also refers to the future, since it anticipates and prophesies the paschal joy which will always fill the Church in view of the ultimate victory of justice and peace at the end of time (cf. *Lk* 1:51-53).

The *Magnificat* is not only vocal prayer. It is also a deep meditation on the history of salvation and a radiant contemplation of the love of God which triumphs in humility. Mary's jubilant song is also the song of her life, a beautiful expression of who she is in Christ.

In an analogous way, the Rosary is a faith-filled contemplation of the mysteries of salvation, with reference to past, present and future. The Rosary includes many aspects of prayer: thanksgiving, petition, love and reparation. It is at once vocal, mental and contemplative prayer. The Rosary is a 'living prayer' which shapes the person who prays it with perseverance; it becomes the prayer of their life, of their vocation in Christ. As such, the Rosary is indeed, as the Holy Father teaches, "a school of prayer, a school of faith".[16]

Recent Popes have described the Rosary as a "compendium of the Gospel".[17] It is an eminently scriptural prayer since the mysteries of the Rosary "awaken in the soul a thirst for a knowledge of Christ continually nourished by the pure source of the Gospel".[18] For this reason St John Paul II suggests that the contemplation of each mystery can be enhanced by "*the proclamation of a related Biblical passage*".[19]

While being a "typically meditative prayer",[20] the Rosary is sustained by the repetition of vocal prayers. As Paul VI expressed it in his 1974 Apostolic Exhortation on devotion to Our Lady: "The succession of Hail Mary's is the warp on which is woven the contemplation of the mysteries".[21] To the objection sometimes made that it is too repetitive, St John Paul II suggests that "to understand the Rosary, one has to enter into the psychological dynamic proper to love".[22] The same point is made by another great contemporary apostle of the Rosary, St Josemaría Escrivá: "But in the Rosary…we always say the same things. Always the same? And don't people in love always say the same things to one another…?"[23]

## The Rosary as a powerful prayer for God's family

The second mystery of light places us in Cana of Galilee. It is wonderful to consider that Our Lord worked his first miracle at a wedding feast, and at the prompting of his Mother. This fact speaks volumes about the joy of the Gospel, the beauty of married love and human celebration, and also about the power of Mary's intercession. When Our Lady first intimates her request to Jesus - "They have no wine" (*Jn* 2:3), the Lord seems to suggest that her petition is premature - "My hour has not yet come" (v. 4). But the Mother's intercession proves entirely effective.

In a truly maternal way, Mary's intervention brings about great benefits for each and all of her children at Cana. The evangelist concludes his account of the miracle in these words: "This, the first of his signs, Jesus did at Cana in Galilee, and manifested his glory, and his disciples believed in him" (v. 11). Everyone has gained from Mary's care: the newlyweds are spared lasting embarrassment, the steward of the feast is unwittingly saved from disgrace, the wedding guests continue to enjoy wine and of the finest quality, Christ begins to show his divinity and his disciples begin to have faith in him.

As Joseph Ratzinger - Benedict XVI - has shown, the event at Cana is also a foreshadowing of Christ's overwhelming love on Calvary where he will pour out the rich wine of his blood for our eternal celebration of the new and everlasting Marriage-Covenant.[24] And, central to this paschal mystery is Our Lady, Mother of Jesus and of his Spouse, the Church.

The power of the Rosary derives from Our Lady's role in salvation history. God has decided to give us Christ through Mary. Hence all good things, every grace, comes through her. As Benedict XVI put it during his 2007 visit to Brazil, "there is no fruit of grace in the history of salvation that does not have as its necessary instrument the mediation of Our Lady".[25]

The efficacy of Mary's intercession, which is a particular sharing in the one mediation of Jesus Christ (cf. *1 Tm* 2:5), is why the Rosary has always been a powerful weapon for goodness and love throughout history.[26] For this reason we continuously "hand over our burdens to the merciful hearts of Christ and his Mother" through the Rosary.[27] Pope Francis has referred to what he calls the "suffering dimension" of the Rosary, as "a sustaining prayer in the battle against the evil one and his accomplices".[28] At the conclusion of an Angelus address in St Peter's Square, the Holy Father encouraged the multitude of people present to take "a special medicine" with them as they departed.[29] Thousands of rosary beads were being distributed among the crowds. The Rosary strengthens us on our journey towards heaven. It is, says Benedict XVI, "the prayer of the Christian who advances on his pilgrimage of faith, following Jesus, preceded by Mary".[30]

Given its power as an expression of Mary's motherly love, the Church has always cherished the Rosary as a great family prayer. The Rosary is, in Pope Francis's words, "communion around the Mother".[31] This prayer brings the children of God together with Christ and one another and hence builds the Church.[32] It is natural, then, that the Rosary is often prayed for the intentions of the Pope, the common Father of God's family. Similarly, the Rosary is frequently offered for peace and for the family. "*The Rosary is by its nature a prayer for peace*", says St John Paul II.[33] And he added that it is also "*a prayer of and for the family*".[34] It is small wonder that the Popes have again and again recommended the family Rosary.[35] In his homily at the Family Day of the Year of Faith, Pope Francis challenged the thousands of families present: "I would like to ask you dear families: Do you pray together from time to time as a family?...Praying the Rosary together, as a family, is very beautiful and a source of great strength".[36]

## The present text

What follows is a series of meditations, one for each of the twenty mysteries of the Holy Rosary. Each reflection is composed of various texts drawn from the preaching of Benedict XVI, which is rightly valued as a treasure-trove of teaching and prayer.

Because "the Rosary is a contemplative and Christocentric prayer, inseparable from meditation on holy

Scripture",[37] each meditation begins with a short Biblical text. In most cases, these words of Scripture figure in the passage taken from Pope Benedict's teaching. In other cases, an appropriate scriptural text has been added. Indeed, characteristic of Benedict XVI's reflections on the mysteries of salvation is the fact that they are scripturally rooted. His words invite us to use our imagination to contemplate the scene we are considering in each mystery.

Benedict XVI's preaching also brings to life many great aspects of the Catholic Faith, such as the Person of Christ, and of Mary, the mystery of the Church and the sacraments, especially Baptism, Penance and the Eucharist, the universal call to holiness and to joyful evangelisation, and the ultimate destiny of eternal life.

Each meditation ends with a petition to the Lord through the intercession of his Mother and ours.

The objective of this selection of reflections is to help enhance meditation on the mysteries of salvation in the Rosary. The texts might be read through as spiritual reading, or taken singly for a period of mental prayer or Eucharistic adoration. They might also be used, or parts of them, in a more prolonged recitation of the Rosary.

# The Joyful Mysteries

## The Annunciation

When God called Mary **"full of grace"** (*Lk* 1:28) the hope of salvation for the human race was enkindled: a daughter of our people found grace in the Lord's eyes, he chose her as Mother of the Redeemer. In the simplicity of Mary's home, in a poor village of Galilee, the solemn prophecy of salvation began to be fulfilled […] Without violence but with the meek courage of her "yes", the Virgin freed us, not from an earthly enemy but from the ancient adversary, by giving a human body to the One who was to crush his head once and for all.

This is why Mary shines on the sea of life and history as a Star of Hope. She does not shine with her own light, but reflects the light of Christ, the Sun who appeared on humanity's horizon so that in following the Star of Mary we can steer ourselves on the journey and keep on the route towards Christ, especially in dark and stormy moments.[38]

"*Full of grace*" […] is Mary's most beautiful name, the name God himself gave to her to indicate that she has always been and will always be the *beloved*, the elect, the one chosen to welcome the most precious gift, Jesus: the incarnate love of God […] Jesus Christ […] is the Source

AVE GRATIA PLENA DOMINVS TECVM (Lc.1,28)

of the *grace* which filled Mary from the very first moment of her existence. She welcomed Jesus with faith and gave him to the world with love. This is also our vocation and our mission, the vocation and mission of the Church: to welcome Christ into our lives and give him to the world, so "that the world might be saved through him" (Jn 3:17).[39]

To transform the world, God chose a humble young girl from a village in Galilee, Mary of Nazareth, and challenged her with this greeting: "Hail, full of grace, the Lord is with you" [...] God repeats them to the Church, to each one of us: Rejoice, the Lord is close! With Mary's help, let us offer ourselves with humility and courage so that the world may accept Christ, who is the source of true joy.[40] When Mary received the angel's visit, she was a young girl from Nazareth leading the simple and courageous life typical of the women of her village. And if God's gaze focussed particularly upon her, trusting in her, Mary wants to tell you once more that not one of you is indifferent in God's eyes. He directs his loving gaze upon each one of you and he calls you to a life that is happy and full of meaning. Do not allow yourselves to be discouraged by difficulties! Mary was disturbed by the message of the angel who came to tell her that she would become the Mother of the Saviour. She was conscious of her frailty in the face of God's omnipotence. Nevertheless, she said "yes", without hesitating. And thanks to her yes, salvation came into the world, thereby changing the history of mankind [...] Do not be afraid to say yes to the Lord's summons when he invites you to walk in his footsteps. Respond generously to the Lord! Only he can fulfil the deepest aspirations of your heart.

Let us ask Mary to teach us how to become, like her, inwardly free, so that in openness to God we may find true freedom, true life, genuine and lasting joy.[41]

## The Visitation

**Mary "arose and went with haste into the hill country"**, to visit Elizabeth (*Lk* 1:39). With these words the evangelist wishes to emphasise that for Mary to follow her own vocation in docility to God's Spirit, who has brought about within her the Incarnation of the Word, means taking a new road and immediately setting out from home, allowing herself to be led on a journey by God alone.

St Ambrose, commenting on Mary's "haste", says: "the grace of the Holy Spirit admits of no delay". Our Lady's life is guided by another: "Behold, I am the handmaid of the Lord; let it be done to me according to your word" (*Lk* 1:38); it is modelled by the Holy Spirit, it is marked by events and encounters, such as that with Elizabeth, but above all by her very special relationship with her Son, Jesus. It is a journey on which Mary, cherishing and pondering in her heart the events of her own life, perceives in them ever more profoundly the mysterious design of God the Father for the salvation of the world.[42]

In Nazareth she received the announcement of her unique motherhood and, immediately after conceiving Jesus by the power of the Holy Spirit, she was impelled by the same Spirit of love to go and help her elderly kinswoman Elizabeth, who had reached the sixth month of a pregnancy that was also miraculous. The young Mary who is carrying Jesus in her womb and, forgetting herself, hurries to the help of her neighbour, is a wonderful image of the Church in the perennial youthfulness of the Spirit, of the missionary Church of the incarnate Word called to bring him to the world and to witness to him especially in the service of charity.[43]

Just as Mary travelled through the hill country of Judah, to share with her kinswoman the joyful news of Christ's coming, so too the Church is called to journey through history, proclaiming the wondrous message of salvation.[44]

Before and more than all the saints, divine charity filled the heart of the Virgin Mary. After the Annunciation, moved by the One she carried in her womb, the Mother of the Word-made-flesh hurriedly set out to visit and help her cousin Elizabeth.[45]

We cannot keep solely for ourselves this joy that we have received; joy must always be shared. Joy must be communicated. Mary went without delay to communicate her joy to her cousin Elizabeth. And ever since her Assumption into heaven she has showered joy upon the whole world, she has become the great Consoler: our

Mother who communicates joy, trust and kindness and also invites us to spread joy [...]

We can transmit this joy simply: with a smile, with a kind gesture, with some small help, with forgiveness. Let us give this joy and the joy given will be returned to us. Let us seek in particular to communicate the deepest joy, that of knowing God in Christ. Let us pray that this presence of God's liberating joy will shine out in our lives.[46]

The Virgin Mary, who did not communicate to the world an idea but Jesus, the Incarnate Word, is an unparalleled model of evangelisation. Let us invoke her with trust so that, in our time too, the Church may proclaim Christ, the Saviour. May every Christian and every community feel the joy of sharing with others the Good News that "God so loved the world that he gave his Only Son...that the world might be saved through him" (*Jn* 3:16-17).[47]

## The Birth of our Lord

**"The time came for Mary to be delivered. And she gave birth to her first-born son and wrapped him in swaddling clothes, and laid him in a manger, because there was no room for them in the inn"** (*Lk* 2:6f.) [...] We can imagine the kind of interior preparation, the kind of love with which Mary approached that hour. The brief phrase: "She wrapped him in swaddling clothes" allows us to glimpse something of the holy joy and the silent zeal of that preparation.[48]

The child lying in the manger is truly God's Son. God is not eternal solitude, but rather a circle of love and mutual self-giving. He is Father, Son and Holy Spirit. But there is more: in Jesus Christ, the Son of God, God himself, God from God, became man.[49]

Although the child lying in a manger looks like all children in the world, at the same time he is totally different: he is the Son of God, he is God, true God and true man. This mystery [...] is great and certainly far from easy to understand with the human mind alone.

Yet, by learning from Mary, we can understand with our hearts what our eyes and minds do not manage to perceive or contain on their own [...] It is precisely on this journey of faith that Mary comes to meet us as our support and guide.[50]

In the stable at Bethlehem, heaven and earth meet. Heaven has come down to Earth. For this reason, a light shines from the stable for all times; for this reason joy is enkindled there; for this reason song is born there.[51]

The Child of Bethlehem reveals and communicates to us the true "Face" of a good and faithful God, who loves us and even in death does not abandon us.[52]

The God we contemplate in the crib is God-Love.[53]

God has made himself small for us. God comes not with external force, but he comes in the powerlessness of his love, which is where his true strength lies. He places himself in our hands. He asks for our love. He invites us to become small ourselves, to come down from our high thrones and to learn to be childlike before God. He speaks to us informally. He asks us to trust him and thus to learn how to live in truth and love.[54]

The Creator who holds all things in his hands, on whom we all depend, makes himself small and in need of human love. God is in the stable [...] How, indeed, could his love for humanity, his solicitude for us, have appeared greater and more pure? [...] For nothing can be more sublime, nothing greater than the love which thus stoops down, descends, becomes dependent. The glory of the true God becomes visible when the eyes of our hearts are opened before the stable of Bethlehem.[55]

The child Jesus who lays in the grotto is the only-begotten Son of God who became man. He will save humanity by dying on the Cross. Now we see him in swaddling clothes in the manger; after his crucifixion he will be clad anew in bandages and laid in a sepulchre.[56]

If Jesus was not born on earth, humankind could not be born unto heaven. Specifically, because Christ is born, we can be "reborn"![57]

God makes himself man and man is given the unheard-of possibility to be a son of God.[58]

May the Virgin Mary, who welcomed Jesus with faith, help us not to close our hearts to his Gospel of salvation. Rather, let us allow ourselves to be conquered and transformed by him, the 'Emmanuel', God who came to dwell among us to offer us the gift of his peace and his love.[59]

## The Presentation of the Child Jesus in the Temple

**"Lift up your heads, O gates! And be lifted up, O ancient doors! That the King of Glory may come in"** (*Ps* 24:7)

But who is the powerful God who enters the temple? It is a child; it is the Infant Jesus in the arms of his Mother, the Virgin Mary.[60]

Jesus enters the ancient temple; he who is the new Temple of God: he comes to visit his people, thus bringing to fulfilment obedience to the Law and ushering the last times of salvation.

It is interesting to take a close look at this entrance of the child Jesus into the solemnity of the temple, in the great comings and goings of many people, busy with their work: priests and Levites taking turns to be on duty, the numerous devout people and pilgrims anxious to encounter the Holy God of Israel. Yet none of them noticed anything. Jesus was a child like the others, a first-born son of very simple parents. Even the priests proved incapable of recognising the signs of the new and special presence of the Messiah and Saviour.[61]

The ritual act of Jesus's parents, which takes place in the humble, hidden manner characteristic of the Incarnation of the Son of God, finds a unique welcome in the elderly Simeon and the prophetess Anna.

Alone two elderly people, Simeon and Anna, discover this great newness. Led by the Holy Spirit, in this child they find the fulfilment of their long waiting and watchfulness.

They both contemplate the light of God that comes to illuminate the world, and their prophetic gaze is opened to the future in the proclamation of the Messiah: "*Lumen ad revelationem gentium!*" (*Lk* 2:32). The prophetic attitude of the two elderly people contains the entire Old Covenant which expresses the joy of the encounter with the Redeemer. Upon seeing the child, Simeon and Anna understood that he was the Awaited One [...]

The Presentation of Jesus in the Temple demonstrates the wisdom of Simeon and Anna, the wisdom of a life completely dedicated to the search for God's face, for his signs, for his will; a life dedicated to listening to and proclaiming his word: "Your face, Lord, do I seek" (*Ps* 27[26]:8).[62]

The first person to be associated with Christ on the path of obedience, proven faith and shared suffering was his Mother, Mary. The Gospel text portrays her in the act of offering her Son: an unconditional offering that involves her in the first person.

Mary is the Mother of the One who is "the glory of [his] people Israel" and a "light for revelation to the Gentiles", but also "a sign that is spoken against" (cf. *Lk* 2:32, 34). And in her immaculate soul, she herself was to be pierced by the sword of sorrow, thus showing that her role in the history of salvation did not end in the mystery of the Incarnation, but was completed in loving and sorrowful participation in the death and Resurrection of her Son.

Bringing her Son to Jerusalem, the Virgin Mother offered him to God as a true Lamb who takes away the sins of the world.[63]

Mary is the Mother who [...] presents her Son to the Father at the Temple, also continuing in this action the "yes" she spoke at the moment of the Annunciation.[64] Mary is the Mother who "shows us the way", giving us Jesus, the "Way of Peace".[65]

## The Finding of the Child Jesus in the Temple

**"Did you not know that I must be in my Father's house?"** (*Lk* 2:49)

The twelve-year-old Jesus [...] stays behind in the Temple in Jerusalem unbeknown to his parents who, surprised and anxious, discover him three days later conversing with the teachers. Jesus answers his Mother, who asks for an explanation, that he must "be in his Father's house" - that is, God's house (cf. *Lk* 2: 49). In this episode the boy Jesus appears to us full of zeal for God and for the Temple.

Let us ask ourselves: from whom did Jesus learn love for his Father's affairs? As Son he certainly had an intimate knowledge of his Father, of God, and a profound and permanent relationship with him but, in his own culture he had, of course, learned prayers and love for the Temple and for the institutions of Israel from his parents. We may therefore say that Jesus's decision to stay on at the Temple was above all the result of his close relationship with the Father, but it was also a result of the education he had received from Mary and Joseph.[66]

Jesus was introduced by Mary and Joseph into the religious community and frequented the synagogue of Nazareth. With them, he learned to make the pilgrimage to Jerusalem […]

This Gospel episode reveals the most authentic and profound vocation of the family: that is, to accompany each of its members on the path of the discovery of God and of the plan that he has prepared for him or her.

Mary and Joseph taught Jesus primarily by their example: in his parents he came to know the full beauty of faith, of love for God and for his law, as well as the demands of justice, which is totally fulfilled in love (cf. *Rm* 13:10).

From them he learned that it is necessary first of all to do God's will, and that the spiritual bond is worth more than the bond of kinship.

The Holy Family of Nazareth is truly the 'prototype' of every Christian family which, united in the Sacrament of Marriage and nourished by the Word and the Eucharist, is called to carry out the wonderful vocation and mission of being the living cell not only of society but also of the Church, a sign and instrument of unity for the entire human race.[67]

Here we can glimpse the authentic meaning of Christian education: it is the fruit of a collaboration between educators and God that must always be sought. The Christian family is aware that children are a gift and a project of God. Therefore it cannot consider that it possesses them; rather, in serving God's plan through them, the family is called to educate them in the greatest freedom, which is precisely that of saying "yes" to God in order to do his will.

The Virgin Mary is the perfect example of this "yes".[68]

Let us [...] invoke for every family, especially families in difficulty, the protection of Mary Most Holy and of St Joseph. May they sustain such families so that they can resist the disintegrating forces of a certain contemporary culture which undermines the very foundations of the family institution.

May they help Christian families to be, in every part of the world, living images of God's love.[69]

"HIC EST FILIVS MEVS DILECTVS IN QVO MIHI COMPLACVI" (Mt. III, 17)

# The Mysteries of Light

## The Baptism of our Lord in the Jordan

When Jesus emerged from the waters, the Holy Spirit descended upon him in the form of a dove, while the Father's voice from heaven proclaimed him **"my beloved Son in whom I am well pleased"** (*Mt* 3:17).

The whole mystery of Christ in the world can be summed up in this term: "baptism" [...] The Son of God, who from eternity shares the fullness of life with the Father and the Holy Spirit, was "immersed" in our reality as sinners to make us share in his own life: he was incarnate, he was born like us, he grew up like us and, on reaching adulthood, manifested his mission which began precisely with the "baptism of conversion" administered by John the Baptist. Jesus's first public act, as we have just heard, was to go down into the Jordan, mingling among repentant sinners, in order to receive this baptism. John was naturally reluctant to baptise him, but because this was the Father's will, Jesus insisted (cf. *Mt* 3:13-15).[70]

Christ's entire mission is summed up in this: to baptise us in the Holy Spirit, to free us from the slavery of death and "to open heaven to us", that is, access to the true and full life that will be "a plunging ever anew into the vastness of being, in which we are simply overwhelmed with joy" [...]

Let us rejoice that the Son of God came to share our human condition, so that we might rise with him to everlasting life.[71]

These words "You are my beloved Son" reveal what eternal life is: it is the filial relationship with God, just as Jesus lived it and as he revealed and gave it to us.[72]

Baptism is more than a bath, a purification. It is more than becoming part of a community. It is a new birth, a new beginning in life. […] In Baptism we give ourselves over to Christ - he takes us unto himself, so that we no longer live for ourselves, but through him, with him and in him; so that we live with him and thus for others. In Baptism we surrender ourselves, we place our lives in his hands, and so we can say with St Paul, "It is no longer I who live, but Christ who lives in me."

[..] This is what is new about Baptism: our life now belongs to Christ, and no longer to ourselves. As a result we are never alone, even in death, but are always with the One who lives for ever. In Baptism, in the company of Christ, we have already made that cosmic journey to the very abyss of death. At his side and, indeed, drawn up in his love, we are freed from fear. He enfolds us and carries us wherever we may go - he who is Life itself.[73]

How great is the gift of Baptism! If we were to take this fully into account, our lives would become a continual "thank you". What a joy for Christian parents, who have seen a new creature come into being from their love, to carry the baby to the baptismal font and see him or her reborn from the womb of the Church, for a life without end! It is a gift, a joy, but also a responsibility! Parents, in fact, together with godparents, must educate their children in accordance with the Gospel.[74]

We pray for all Christians, so that they may understand the gift of Baptism ever more and apply themselves to live it coherently, witnessing to the love of the Father and of the Son and of the Holy Spirit.[75]

## The Wedding Feast at Cana

**"On the third day there was a marriage at Cana in Galilee, and the mother of Jesus was there"** (*Jn* 2:1)

From its beginnings, the Christian community has seen the personification of Israel and Jerusalem in a female figure as an important and prophetic approach to the Virgin Mary, who is recognised precisely as a "daughter of Zion" and the archetype of the people who "found grace" in the eyes of the Lord. This is an interpretation we find again in the Gospel account of the wedding feast at Cana (*Jn* 2:1-11).

The evangelist John sheds symbolic light on the fact that Jesus is the Bridegroom of Israel, the new Israel that all of us are in faith, the spouse who has come to bring the grace of the new Covenant, represented by the "good wine". At the same time the Gospel emphasises Mary's role, who at the beginning is called "the Mother of Jesus" but the Son himself later addresses her as “woman”, and this has a very profound meaning: indeed, it implies that Jesus, to our wonder, before kinship places the spiritual bond according to which Mary herself impersonates the beloved Bride of the Lord, that is, the People he has chosen to shower his blessings upon the whole human family.

The symbol of the wine, together with that of the banquet, re-proposes the theme of joy and of the feast. In addition, the wine, like the other biblical images of the vineyard and the vine, alludes metaphorically to love: God is the owner of the vineyard, Israel is the vineyard, a vineyard that will find its perfect fulfilment in Christ, of whom we are the branches; and the wine is the fruit, that is, love, because it is exactly love that God expects of his children.[76]

Mary is the image and model of all mothers, of their great mission to be guardians of life, of their mission to be teachers of the art of living and of the art of loving.[77]

The closer a person is to God, the closer he is to people. We see this in Mary. The fact that she is totally with God is the reason why she is so close to human beings.

For this reason she can be the Mother of every consolation and every help, a Mother whom anyone can dare to address in any kind of need in weakness and in sin, for she has understanding for everything and is for everyone the open power of creative goodness [...]

Mary thus stands before us as a sign of comfort, encouragement and hope. She turns to us, saying: "Have the courage to dare with God! Try it! Do not be afraid of him! Have the courage to risk with faith! Have the courage to risk with goodness! Have the courage to risk with a pure heart! Commit yourselves to God, then you will see that it is precisely by doing so that your life will become broad and light, not boring but filled with infinite surprises, for God's infinite goodness is never depleted!"[78]

From Mary we learn graciousness and readiness to help, but we also learn humility and generosity in accepting God's will, in the confident conviction that, whatever it may be, it will be our, and my own, true good.[79]

May she help us to respond constantly and joyously to the Lord's call and to find our happiness in toiling for the Kingdom of Heaven.[80]

## The Proclamation of the Kingdom and the Call to Conversion

The "Good News" which Jesus proclaims is summed up in this sentence: **"The Kingdom of God - or Kingdom of Heaven - is at hand"** (cf. *Mt* 4:17; *Mk* 1:15). What do these words mean? They do not, of course, refer to an earthly region marked out in space and time, but rather to an announcement that it is God who reigns, that God is Lord and that his lordship is present and actual, it is being realised.

The newness of Christ's message, therefore, is that God made himself close *in him* and now reigns in our midst, as the miracles and healings that he works demonstrate. God reigns in the world through his Son made man and with the power of the Holy Spirit who is called "the finger of God" (*Lk* 11:20). Wherever Jesus goes, the Creator Spirit brings life, and men and women are healed of diseases of body and spirit. God's lordship is thus manifest in the human being's integral healing.

By this, Jesus wanted to reveal the face of the true God, the God who is close, full of mercy for every human being; the God who makes us a gift of life in abundance, his own life. The Kingdom of God is therefore life that asserts itself over death, the light of truth that dispels the darkness of ignorance and lies.

Jesus began his preaching in Galilee, the region where he grew up, the 'outskirts' in comparison with the heart of the Jewish Nation which was Judea, and in it, Jerusalem. But the prophet Isaiah had foretold that this land, assigned to the tribes of Zebulun and Napthali, would have a glorious future: the people immersed in darkness would see a great light (cf. *Is* 8:23-9: 2) […]

Let us pray to Mary Most Holy that she will always obtain for the Church the same passion for God's Kingdom which enlivened the mission of Jesus Christ: a passion for God, for his lordship of love and life; a passion for man, encountered in truth with the desire to give him the most precious treasure: the love of God, his Creator and Father.[81]

"Repent, and believe in the Gospel" (*Mk* 1:15). Jesus began his public life with this invitation that continues to resonate in the Church to the point that in her apparitions, the Virgin Most Holy has renewed this appeal, especially in recent times. [...] Let us think in particular of Fatima, where [...] from 13th May to 13th October 1917, the Virgin appeared to the three little shepherd children: Lucia, Jacinta and Francisco.[82]

Conversion overcomes the root of evil, which is sin, even if it cannot always avoid its consequences.[83]

The Sacrament of Confession [is] a true encounter with God's love, which every person needs in order to live in joy and peace.[84]

The Sacrament of Reconciliation [...] in the deepest sense of the word is a sacrament of healing. The real wound in the soul, in fact, the reason for all our other injuries, is sin. And only if forgiveness exists, by virtue of God's power, by virtue of Christ's love, can we be healed, can we be redeemed.[85]

Let us pray to Mary Most Holy, who accompanies and sustains us [...], so that she may help every Christian to rediscover the greatness, I would say, the beauty, of conversion.[86]

May the Virgin Mary guide us to true conversion of heart, so that we may make the necessary choices to harmonise our mentalities with the Gospel.[87]

## The Transfiguration of our Lord

**"He took with him Peter and John and James, and went up on the mountain to pray"** (*Lk* 9:28).

Jesus went up on the mountain "to pray" (9:28), together with the apostles Peter, James and John, and it was "while he prayed" (9:29) that the luminous mystery of his Transfiguration occurred. Thus, for the three apostles, going up the mountain meant being involved in the prayer of Jesus, who frequently withdrew in prayer especially at dawn and after sunset, and sometimes all night.

However, this was the only time, on the mountain, that he chose to reveal to his friends the inner light that filled him when he prayed: his face, we read in the Gospel, shone and his clothes were radiant with the splendour of the divine Person of the Incarnate Word (cf. *Lk* 9: 29).[88]

I wish to emphasise that the Transfiguration of Jesus was essentially an experience of prayer (cf. *Lk* 9: 28-29). Indeed, prayer reaches its culmination and thus becomes a source of inner light when the spirit of the human being adheres to that of God and their respective wills merge, as it were, to become a whole. When Jesus went up the mountain, he was immersed in contemplation of the loving plan of the Father, who had sent him into the world to save humanity. Elijah and Moses appeared beside Jesus, meaning that the Sacred Scriptures were in concordance with the proclamation of his Paschal Mystery; that in other words Christ had to suffer and die in order to enter into his glory (cf. *Lk* 24:26,46). At that moment Jesus saw silhouetted before him the Cross, the extreme sacrifice necessary in order to free us from the dominion of sin and death. And in his heart, once again, he repeated his "Amen". He said yes, here I am, may your loving will be done, O Father. And as had happened after his Baptism in the Jordan, from heaven there came signs of God the Father's pleasure: the light that transfigured Christ and the voice that proclaimed him "my beloved Son" (*Mk* 9:7).[89]

Prayer is not an accessory or 'optional', but a question of life or death. In fact, only those who pray, in other words, who entrust themselves to God with filial love, can enter eternal life, which is God himself.[90]

The Transfiguration is a prayer event: in praying, Jesus is immersed in God, closely united to him, adhering with his own human will to the loving will of the Father, and thus light invades him and appears visibly as the truth of his being: he is God, Light of Light. Even Jesus's raiment becomes dazzling white [...] This is the crucial point: the Transfiguration is an anticipation of the Resurrection, but this presupposes death [...]

Jesus wanted his disciples, in particular those who would be responsible for guiding the nascent Church, to have a direct experience of his divine glory, so that they could face the scandal of the Cross. Indeed, when the hour of betrayal came and Jesus withdrew to the Garden of

Gethsemane, he kept the same disciples Peter, James and John close to him, asking them to watch and pray with him (cf. *Mt* 26:38).[91]

On the transfigured face of Jesus a ray of light which he held within shines forth. This same light was to shine on Christ's face on the day of the Resurrection. In this sense, the Transfiguration appears as a foretaste of the Paschal Mystery.[92]

Turning in prayer to Mary, let us recognise in her the human creature transfigured within by Christ's grace and entrust ourselves to her guidance, to walk joyfully on our path.[93]

Let us ask Mary, Mother of the Incarnate Word and Teacher of the spiritual life, to teach us to pray as her Son did so that our life may be transformed by the light of his presence.[94]

## The Institution of the Holy Eucharist

**"This is my body which is given for you. Do this in remembrance of me"** (*Lk* 22:19).

In the Upper Room the mystery of grace and salvation, of which we are recipients and also heralds and ministers, can be expressed only in terms of love. Because he has loved us first and continues to do so, we can respond with love. Our life as Christians is not simply a human effort to live the demands of the Gospel imposed upon us as duties. In the Eucharist we are drawn into the mystery of divine love. Our lives become a grateful, docile and active acceptance of the power of a love which is given to us.[95]

The *berakah*, Israel's prayer of blessing and thanksgiving, has become our Eucharistic celebration in which the Lord blesses our gifts - the bread and wine - to give himself in them.[96]

At the Last Supper, on the night before his death on the Cross, Jesus instituted the sacrament of the new and eternal covenant between God and man. May this sacrifice of reconciliation, in which the Risen Lord is truly and substantially present under the appearances of Bread and Wine, confirm the Church in faith, unity and holiness as she awaits his future coming in glory.[97]

The Last Supper is the locus of the nascent Church, the womb containing the Church of every age. In the Eucharist, Christ's sacrifice is constantly renewed, Pentecost is constantly renewed.[98]

Mary, present on Calvary beneath the Cross, is also present with the Church and as Mother of the Church in each one of our Eucharistic celebrations. No one better than she, therefore, can teach us to understand and live Holy Mass with faith and love, uniting ourselves with Christ's redeeming sacrifice.[99]

May Mary, who bearing Jesus in her womb was the first living 'tabernacle' of the Eucharist, communicate to us her same faith in the holy mystery of the Body and Blood of her divine Son, so that it may truly be the centre of our life.[100]

May the Virgin Mary, the Woman of the Eucharist, introduce us into the secret of true adoration. Her humble and simple heart was ever pondering the mystery of Jesus, in whom she adored the presence of God and of his redeeming love.[101]

Let us pray that he will increasingly draw us to himself with Holy Communion. Let us pray that he will help us not to keep our life for ourselves, but to give it to him and thus to work with him so that people may find life: the true life which can only come from the One who himself is the Way, the Truth and the Life.[102]

When we receive Holy Communion, like Mary and united to her, we too clasp the wood that Jesus with his love transformed into an instrument of salvation, and pronounce our "Amen" our "Yes" to Love, crucified and risen.[103]

May faith in the Eucharistic Mystery, joy in participating in Holy Mass, especially on Sundays, and enthusiasm in witnessing to Christ's immense love grow throughout the Church through her intercession.[104]

You, Mary, who were the woman "of the Eucharist" throughout your life, help us to walk united towards the heavenly goal, nourished by the Body and Blood of Christ, the eternal Bread of life and medicine of divine immortality. Amen![105]

# The Sorrowful Mysteries

## The Agony in the Garden

**"Abba, Father, all things are possible to thee; remove this cup from me"** (*Mk* 14:36).

On the Mount of Olives, at the moment of Jesus's extreme anguish, the disciples, before falling asleep, had heard him talking to the Father and calling him "*Abbà* Father". This is a very familiar word equivalent to our 'Daddy', used only by children in talking to their father. Until that time it had been unthinkable for a Jew to use such a word in order to address God; but Jesus, being a true Son, at that moment of intimacy used this form and said: "Abba, Father". Surprisingly, in St Paul's Letters to the Romans and to the Galatians, this word 'Abba', that expresses the exclusivity of Jesus's sonship, appears on the lips of the baptised (cf. *Rm* 8:15; *Ga* 4:6) because they have received the "Spirit of the Son". They now carry this Spirit within them and can speak like Jesus and with Jesus as true children to their Father; they can say "Abba" because they have become sons in the Son.[106]

Prostrated by extreme anguish because of the death that was hanging over him, Jesus offers up prayers and supplications to God "with loud cries and tears" (*Heb* 5:7).

ET FACT
PROLIXIVS

He invokes help from the One who can set him free but always remaining abandoned in the Father's hands. And precisely because of his filial trust in God [...] he was heard, in the sense that he was raised, he received new and definitive life. The Letter to the Hebrews makes us understand that these insistent prayers, of Jesus with tears and cries, were the true act of the High Priest with which he offered himself and humanity to the Father, thereby transforming the world.[107]

In that hour Jesus did not doubt in the power of God the Father or in his closeness, even though he had to experience to the full the distance of hatred from love, of falsehood from the truth, of sin from grace. He experienced this drama in himself with excruciating pain, especially in Gethsemane, before his arrest, and then throughout his Passion until his death on the Cross. In that hour, Jesus on the one hand was one with the Father, fully abandoned to him; on the other, since he showed solidarity to sinners, he was as it were separated and felt abandoned by him.[108]

It was the Father's love that permitted the Son to confidently face his last "baptism", which he himself defines as the apex of his mission (cf. *Lk* 12:50). Jesus received that baptism of sorrow and love for us, for all of humanity. He has suffered for truth and justice, bringing the Gospel of suffering to human history, which is the other aspect of the Gospel of love. God cannot suffer, but he can and wants to be compassionate. Through Christ's passion he can bring his *con-solatio* to every human suffering, "the consolation of God's compassionate love - and so the star of hope rises" (*Spe Salvi*, n. 39).[109]

Let us invoke the help of the Blessed Virgin who followed Jesus first and to the very end on the way of the Cross. May she help us to walk in the Lord's footsteps with determination, to experience from this moment, even in trial, the glory of the Resurrection.[110]

## The Scourging at the Pillar

**"This is my blood of the covenant, which is poured out for many for the forgiveness of sins"** (*Mt* 26:28) [...] From the scourging to the piercing of his side after his death on the Cross, Christ poured out all his Blood as the true Lamb sacrificed for the redemption of all [...]

Christ did not respond to evil with evil, but with goodness, with his infinite love. The blood of Christ is the pledge of God's faithful love for humanity. Every human being, even in conditions of extreme moral wretchedness can say, fixing his eyes on the wounds of the Crucified One: "God has not abandoned me, he loves me, he has given his life for me", and thus rediscover hope.[111]

St John writes: "Having loved his own who were in the world, he loved them to the end" (*Jn* 13:1). By virtue of this oblative and total love we are radically ransomed from sin, as St John writes further: "My little children...if any one does sin, we have an advocate with the Father, Jesus

Christ, the righteous; and he is the expiation for our sins, and not for ours only, but also for the sins of the whole world"(*1 Jn* 2:1-2; cf. *1 Jn* 1:7).

This is how Jesus's love for us reaches us: by the pouring out of his own blood for our salvation! The Christian, pausing in contemplation before this "excess" of love, cannot but wonder what the proper response is. And I think each one of us, always and over and over again, must ask himself or herself this.[112]

May divine grace open our hearts to an understanding of the invaluable gift of salvation, obtained for us by Christ's sacrifice.[113]

The Lord took his wounds with him to eternity. He is a wounded God; he let himself be injured through his love for us. His wounds are a sign for us that he understands and allows himself to be wounded out of love for us.

These wounds of his: how tangible they are to us in the history of our time! Indeed, time and again he allows himself to be wounded for our sake. What certainty of his mercy, what consolation do his wounds mean for us! And what security they give us regarding his identity: "My Lord and my God!" And what a duty they are for us, the duty to allow ourselves in turn to be wounded for him![114]

God has suffered, and through his Son he suffers with us. This is the summit of his power, that he can suffer with us. In this way he demonstrates the true divine power: he desired to suffer with us and for us. In our suffering we are never left alone. God, through his Son, suffered first, and he is close to us in our suffering.[115]

May the Virgin Mary, who at the foot of the Cross together with the apostle John received the testament of Jesus' blood, help us to rediscover the inestimable richness of this grace and to feel deep and everlasting gratitude for it.[116]

## The Crowning with Thorns

**"For this I was born, and for this I have come into the world, to bear witness to the truth. Everyone who is of the truth hears my voice"** (*Jn* 18: 37).

But what is the 'truth' that Christ came into the world to witness to? The whole of his life reveals that God is love: so this is the truth to which he witnessed to the full with the sacrifice of his own life on Calvary.[117]

In what does this 'power' of Jesus Christ the King consist? It is not the power of the kings or the great people of this world; it is the divine power to give eternal life, to liberate from evil, to defeat the dominion of death. It is the power of Love that can draw good from evil, that can melt a hardened heart, bring peace amid the harshest conflict and kindle hope in the thickest darkness. This Kingdom of Grace is never imposed and always respects our freedom. Christ came "to bear witness to the truth" (Jn 18: 37), as he declared to Pilate.[118]

It seems paradoxical: Christ has not enriched us with his richness but with his poverty, with his love that brought him to give himself totally to us.[119]

Let us not distance our hearts from this mystery of profound humanity and lofty spirituality. Looking at Christ, we feel at the same time looked at by him. He whom we have pierced with our faults never tires of pouring out upon the world an inexhaustible torrent of merciful love.

May humankind understand that only from this font is it possible to draw the indispensable spiritual energy to build that peace and happiness which every human being continually seeks.[120]

May the infinite love of Christ that shines in his face be radiant in your every attitude, and become your 'daily life'. As St Augustine urged in an Easter homily, "Christ has suffered; let us die to sin. Christ is risen; let us live for God. Christ has passed from this world to the Father; let us not be attached to this earth with our hearts but follow him in the things of above. Our Lord was hung on the wood of the Cross; let us crucify concupiscence of the flesh. He lay in the tomb; buried with him, let us forget past things; he is seated in heaven; let us concentrate our longing on our desires to supreme things".[121]

Let us pray for those who suffer for being faithful to Christ and to his Church.[122]

Let us […] invoke the motherly intercession of Mary, so that our life may become a reflection of Christ's. Let us pray that all those whom we meet may always perceive in our gestures and in our words the pacifying and comforting goodness of his face.[123]

## The Carrying of the Cross

**"If any man would come after me, let him deny himself and take up his cross and follow me"** (*Mk* 8: 34).

His is a death that puts an end to death; the way of the Cross leads to Resurrection.[124]

The way of the Cross is in fact the only way that leads to the victory of love over hatred, of sharing over selfishness, of peace over violence.[125]

Yes [...] the Cross is the definitive revelation of love and divine mercy for us as well, men and women of this epoch, all too often distracted by earthly and transient apprehensions and concerns.

God is love, and his love is the secret of our happiness. So it is that there is no other way to enter into this mystery of love than to lose ourselves, to give ourselves: the way of the Cross.[126]

Jesus's invitation to take up one's cross and follow him may at first sight seem harsh and contrary to what we hope for, mortifying our desire for personal fulfilment. At a closer look, however, we discover that it is not like this: the witness of the saints shows that in the Cross of Christ, in the love that is given, in renouncing the possession of oneself, one finds that deep serenity which is the source of generous dedication to our brethren, especially to the poor and the needy, and this also gives us joy.[127]

It is not enough to believe that he is God but that, impelled by charity, it is necessary to follow him on the same path, that of the Cross (cf. *Mk* 8:31-33). Jesus did not come to teach us philosophy but to show us a way, indeed the way that leads to life.[128]

The theology of the Cross is not a theory; it is the reality of Christian life. To live in the belief in Jesus Christ, to live in truth and love implies daily sacrifice, implies suffering. Christianity is not the easy road, it is, rather, a difficult climb, but one illuminated by the light of Christ and by the great hope that is born of him.[129]

In order to bring the work of salvation fully to completion, the Redeemer continues to associate to himself and his mission men and women who are prepared to take up their cross and follow him. Consequently, just as for Christ carrying the Cross was not an option, but a mission to be embraced for love, so it is for Christians too. In our world today, where the forces that divide and destroy seem to dominate, Christ does not cease to offer to all his clear invitation: anyone who wants to be my disciple must renounce his own selfishness and carry the Cross with me.[130]

Spiritually united to Our Lady of Sorrows, let us also renew our "yes" to God who chose the way of the Cross in order to save us. This is a great mystery which continues and will continue to take place until the end of the world, and which also asks for our collaboration.

May Mary help us to take up our cross every day and follow Jesus faithfully on the path of obedience, sacrifice and love.[131]

## The Crucifixion and Death of our Lord

**"They crucified him"** (*Jn* 19:18).

The maximum revelation of God possible in this world occurs in Jesus Crucified, because God is love and the death of Jesus on the Cross is the greatest act of love in all of history.[132]

The Crucified One is wisdom, for he truly shows who God is, that is, a force of love which went even as far as the Cross to save men and women. God uses ways and means that seem to us at first sight to be merely weakness. The Crucified One reveals on the one hand man's frailty and on the other, the true power of God, that is the free gift of love: this totally gratuitous love is true wisdom.[133]

The power that comes from the Cross, the power of self-giving goodness - this is the true kingship.[134]

The Crucified Christ embraces the entire universe in all its dimensions.[135]

It is true: the Cross shows "the breadth and length and height and depth" - the cosmic dimensions are the meaning - of a love that surpasses all knowledge, a love that goes beyond what is known and fills us "with all the fullness of God" (*Ep* 3:18-19).[136]

Contemplating the Crucified One with the eyes of faith we can understand in depth what sin is, how tragic is its gravity, and at the same time, how immense is the Lord's power of forgiveness and mercy.[137]

Our own crosses acquire value if we consider them and accept them as a part of the Cross of Christ, if a reflection of his light illuminates them.

It is by that Cross alone that our sufferings too are ennobled and acquire their true meaning.[138]

The sign of the Cross is a kind of synthesis of our faith, for it tells how much God loves us; it tells us that there is a love in this world that is stronger than death, stronger than our weaknesses and sins.[139]

We contemplate Mary sharing her Son's compassion for sinners. As St Bernard declares, the Mother of Christ entered into the Passion of her Son through her compassion. At the foot of the Cross, the prophecy of Simeon is fulfilled: her mother's heart is pierced through (cf. *Lk* 2:35) by the torment inflicted on the Innocent One born of her flesh. Just as Jesus cried (cf. *Jn* 11:35), so too Mary certainly cried over the tortured body of her Son. Her self-restraint, however, prevents us from plumbing the depths of her grief.[140]

Let us therefore turn [...] to you, Virgin Mary, who stood unwavering at the foot of your Son's Cross. You are a model of faith and hope in the power of truth and goodness. With the words of the ancient hymn we invoke you: "Break the fetters of the oppressed, / give light to the blind, / cast all evil from us, / beseech our every good". And [...] we want to entrust to you the peoples [...] of the whole world, invoking development and peace for all: "Grant us peace in our day, / watch over our way, / grant that we may see your Son, / in the fullness of joy in heaven". Amen.[141]

# The Glorious Mysteries

## The Resurrection of our Lord

Jesus's words resound: **"I am risen and I am with you always"** (cf. *Ps* 139:18). Echoing this good news, the Church proclaims exultantly: "Yes, we are certain! The Lord is truly risen, alleluia! The power and the glory are his, now and forever". The whole Church rejoices, expressing her sentiments by singing: "This is the day of Our Lord Jesus Christ". In fact, in rising from the dead, Jesus inaugurated his eternal day and has opened the door to our joy, too. "I will not die", he says, "but will have everlasting life". The crucified Son of man, the stone rejected by the builders, has now become the solid foundation of the new spiritual edifice which is the Church, his mystical Body [...]

It is right for the Christian community to rejoice, all of us, because the Resurrection of the Lord assures us that the divine plan of salvation, despite all the obscurity of history, will certainly be brought about. This is why his Passover truly is our hope. And we, risen with Christ through Baptism, must now follow him faithfully in holiness of life, advancing towards the eternal Passover, sustained by the knowledge that the difficulties, struggles and trials

EGO SVM RESVRRECTIO ET VITA

of human life, including death, henceforth can no longer separate us from him and his love. His Resurrection has formed a bridge between the world and eternal life over which every man and every woman can cross to reach the true goal of our earthly pilgrimage.[142]

"I am risen and I am with you always", the Lord tells us, and my hand supports you. Wherever you may fall, you will fall into my hands and I will be there even to the gates of death. Where no one can accompany you any longer and where you can take nothing with you, there I will wait for you to transform for you the darkness into light.[143]

Christ triumphed over death with the omnipotence of his love. Love alone is omnipotent. This love impelled Christ to die for us and thus to overcome death. Yes, love alone gives access to the Kingdom of life![144]

Christ also conquers sin and death today with his love. Evil in all its forms does not have the last word. The final triumph, the triumph of truth and love, is Christ's![145]

Let us pray: Lord, show us that love is stronger than hatred, that love is stronger than death. Descend into the darkness and the abyss of our modern age, and take by the hand those who await you. Bring them to the light! In my own dark nights, be with me to bring me forth! Help me, help all of us, to descend with you into the darkness of all those people who are still waiting for you, who out of the depths cry unto you! Help us to bring them your light![146]

Jesus is not a character from the past. He lives, and he walks before us as one who is alive, he calls us to follow him, the living one, and in this way to discover for ourselves too the path of life.[147]

The Resurrection […] reveals definitively the real identity and the extraordinary stature of the Crucified One. An incomparable and towering dignity: *Jesus is God!*[148]

*May the Virgin Mary help us to savour to the full the joy of Easter, so that, sustained by the power of the Holy Spirit, we may become capable of spreading it in turn wherever we live and work.*[149]

Yes, Lord, make us Easter people, men and women of light, filled with the fire of your love. Amen.[150]

## The Ascension of our Lord

Our Redeemer who died **"for sins once for all […] has gone into heaven and is at the right hand of God with angels, authorities, and powers subject to him"** (*1 P* 3:18, 22). "Carried up into heaven" and made invisible to the eyes of his disciples, Jesus nevertheless did not abandon them. Indeed, "put to death in the flesh but made alive in the spirit" (*1 P* 3:18), he is now present in a new way, within believers, and in him salvation is offered to every human being independently of his race, language or culture.[151]

In this perspective we understand why the evangelist Luke says that after the Ascension the disciples returned to

Jerusalem "with great joy" (24:52). Their joy stems from the fact that what had happened was not really a separation, the Lord's permanent absence: on the contrary, they were then certain that the Crucified-Risen One was alive and that in him God's gates, the gates of eternal life, had been opened to humanity for ever. In other words, his Ascension did not imply a temporary absence from the world but rather inaugurated the new, definitive and insuppressible form of his presence by virtue of his participation in the royal power of God. It was to be up to them, the disciples emboldened by the power of the Holy Spirit, to make his presence visible by their witness, preaching and missionary zeal [...]

We too, accepting the invitation of the "two men in dazzling apparel", must not stay gazing up at the sky, but, under the guidance of the Holy Spirit must go everywhere and proclaim the saving message of Christ's death and Resurrection. His very words, with which the Gospel according to St Matthew ends, accompany and comfort us: "and lo, I am with you always, to the close of the age" (*Mt* 28:19).[152]

It was for our sake that he came down from heaven and for our sake that he ascended to it, after making himself in all things like men, humbling himself even to death on a cross and after having touched the abyss of the greatest distance from God [...] Therefore, Christian hope, founded on Christ, is not an illusion but, as the Letter to the

Hebrews says, "we have this as a sure and steadfast anchor of the soul" (*Heb* 6:19), an anchor that penetrates heaven where Christ has gone before us.[153]

In Christ ascended into heaven, the human being has entered into intimacy with God in a new and unheard-of way; man henceforth finds room in God for ever. 'Heaven': this word heaven does not indicate a place above the stars, but something far more daring and sublime: it indicates Christ himself, the divine Person who welcomes humanity fully and for ever, the One in whom God and man are inseparably united for ever. Man's being in God, this is heaven. And we draw close to heaven, indeed, we enter heaven to the extent that we draw close to Jesus and enter into communion with him.[154]

We are called [...] to renew our faith in Jesus, the only true hope of salvation for all humanity. Ascending to heaven, he reopened the pathway to paradise, our final homeland. Now, with the power of his Spirit, he sustains us in our daily pilgrimage on earth.[155]

Like the apostles then, we too, after the Ascension, gather in prayer to invoke the outpouring of the Spirit in spiritual union with the Virgin Mary (cf. *Ac* 1:12-14). May her intercession obtain a renewed Pentecost for the whole Church.[156]

## The Descent of the Holy Spirit

**"You will receive power when the Holy Spirit comes upon you"** (*Ac* 1:8).

We have seen this promise fulfilled! On the day of Pentecost […] the Risen Lord, seated at the right hand of the Father, sent the Spirit upon the disciples gathered in the Upper Room. In the power of that Spirit, Peter and the apostles went forth to preach the Gospel to the ends of the earth. In every age, and in every language, the Church throughout the world continues to proclaim the marvels of God and to call all nations and peoples to faith, hope and new life in Christ.[157]

On his way up to Jerusalem he had declared to his disciples: "I came to cast fire upon the earth; and would that it were already kindled!" (*Lk* 12:49). These words were most visibly brought about fifty days after the Resurrection, at Pentecost, the ancient Jewish feast which in the Church has become the feast par excellence of the Holy Spirit: "There appeared to them tongues as of fire...and they were all filled with the Holy Spirit" (*Ac* 2:3-4). The real fire, the Holy Spirit, was brought to the earth by Christ […]

This pure, essential and personal "fire", the fire of love, came down upon the apostles gathered in prayer with Mary in the Upper Room, to make the Church an extension of Christ's work of renewal.[158]

In this extraordinary event we find the essential and qualifying characteristics of the Church: the Church is *one*, like the community at Pentecost, who were united in prayer and "concordant": "were of one heart and soul" (*Ac* 4:32).

The Church is *holy*, not by her own merits, but because, animated by the Holy Spirit, she keeps her gaze on Christ, to become conformed to him and to his love.

The Church is *catholic*, because the Gospel is destined for all peoples, and for this, already at the beginning, the Holy Spirit made her speak all languages.

The Church is *apostolic*, because, built upon the foundation of the apostles, she faithfully keeps their teaching through the uninterrupted chain of episcopal succession.

What is more, the Church by her nature is *missionary*, and from the day of Pentecost the Holy Spirit does not cease to move her along the ways of the world to the ends of the earth and to the end of time.[159]

The Church has no boundaries; she is universal. And geographical, cultural, ethnic, and even religious frontiers are an invitation to the Church to evangelise with a view to "communion in diversity". The Church was born at Pentecost, she was born universal and her vocation is to speak all the world's languages. The Church exists, according to her original vocation and mission that were revealed to Abraham, to be a blessing to benefit all the peoples of the earth (cf. *Gn* 12:1-3); to be, in the language of the Second Vatican Council, a sign and instrument of unity for the entire human race.[160]

The Church [...] despite the limitations and sins of men and women, continues to cross the ocean of history, blown by the breath of God and enlivened by his purifying fire.[161]

Let us rediscover the beauty of being baptised in the Holy Spirit; let us recover awareness of our Baptism and our Confirmation, ever timely sources of grace.

May the Virgin of listening, the Mother of the Church obtain [...] for all Christians a renewed outpouring of the Holy Spirit, the Paraclete: "Send forth your Spirit, and they shall be recreated, and you shall renew the face of the earth". Amen.[162]

## The Assumption of Our Lady

**"And a great portent appeared in heaven, a woman clothed with the sun, with the moon under her feet, and on her head a crown of twelve stars"** (*Rv* 12:1).

By contemplating Mary in heavenly glory, we understand that the earth is not the definitive homeland for us either, and that if we live with our gaze fixed on eternal goods we will one day share in this same glory and the earth will become more beautiful.[163]

Caught up in daily activities we risk thinking that here, in this world which we are only passing through, is the ultimate goal of human existence. Instead, paradise is the true goal of our earthly pilgrimage.[164]

Only the prospect of eternity can give authentic value to historical events and especially to the mystery of human frailty, suffering and death.[165] Earthly realities are lived properly because the eternal truth of divine love illuminates them.[166]

Let us, therefore, turn our gaze to Our Lady, Star of Hope, who illumines us on our earthly journey.[167]

Just as Christ rose from the dead with his glorious Body and ascended into heaven, the Holy Virgin, completely united to him, was assumed into heavenly glory in her entire person. In this too, the Mother resembled her Son very closely, leading the way for us.[168]

What a great mystery of love is presented to us […] for our contemplation! Christ triumphed over death with the omnipotence of his love. Love alone is omnipotent […] And Mary entered after her Son, associated with his glory, after being associated with his Passion. She entered it with an uncontainable force, keeping the way behind her open to us all. And for this reason we invoke her today as "Gate of Heaven", "Queen of Angels" and "Refuge of sinners". It is certainly not reasoning that will make us understand this reality which is so sublime, but rather simple, forthright faith and the silence of prayer that puts us in touch with the mystery that infinitely exceeds us […]

Look to Mary, taken up into heaven […] God wins. Faith, which seems weak, is the true force of the world. Love is stronger than hate.[169]

Love has shown that it is stronger than death, that God possesses the true strength and that his strength is goodness and love.[170]

We have a mother in heaven. And the Mother of God, the Mother of the Son of God, is our Mother. He himself has said so. He made her our Mother when he said to the disciple and to all of us: "Behold, your Mother!" We have a Mother in heaven. Heaven is open, heaven has a heart [...]

Mary is taken up body and soul into the glory of heaven, and with God and in God she is Queen of heaven and earth. And is she really so remote from us?

The contrary is true. Precisely because she is with God and in God, she is very close to each one of us. While she lived on this earth she could only be close to a few people. Being in God, who is close to us, actually, 'within' all of us, Mary shares in this closeness of God. Being in God and with God, she is close to each one of us, knows our hearts, can hear our prayers, can help us with her motherly kindness [...]

She always listens to us, she is always close to us, and being Mother of the Son, participates in the power of the Son and in his goodness. We can always entrust the whole of our lives to this Mother, who is not far from any one of us.[171]

May you be praised for ever, O Virgin Mary! Pray the Lord for us.[172]

## The Coronation of Our Lady

**"At your right hand stands the queen in gold of Ophir"** (*Ps* 45:9).

In his eternal Kingdom, God welcomes those who strive day after day to put his Word into practice. For this reason the Virgin Mary, the humblest of all creatures, is the greatest in his eyes and sits as Queen at the right of Christ the King.[173]

The Virgin Mary was associated in a very special way with Christ's kingship. God asked her, a humble young woman of Nazareth, to become Mother of the Messiah and Mary responded to this request with her whole self, joining her unconditional "yes" to that of her Son, Jesus, and making herself obedient with him even in his sacrifice. This is why God exalted her above every other creature and Christ crowned her Queen of heaven and earth.[174]

In Mary Immaculate we contemplate the reflection of the beauty that saves the world: the beauty of God resplendent on the face of Christ. In Mary this beauty is totally pure, humble, free from all pride and presumption.[175]

Let us entrust the Church and all humanity to her intercession, so that God's love can reign in all hearts and his design of justice and peace be fulfilled.[176]

Mary has left death behind her; she is totally clothed in life, she is taken up body and soul into God's glory and thus, placed in glory after overcoming death, she says to us: Take heart, it is love that wins in the end!

The message of my life was: I am the handmaid of God, my life has been a gift of myself to God and my neighbour. And this life of service now arrives in real life. May you too have trust and have the courage to live like this, countering all the threats of the dragon.[177]

What happened in Mary also applies in ways that are different yet real to every man and to every woman because God asks each one of us to welcome him, to put at his disposal our heart and our body, our entire existence [...] so that he may dwell in the world.

He calls us to be united with him in the sacrament of the Eucharist, Bread broken for the life of the world, to form together the Church, his Body in history. And if we say "yes", like Mary, indeed to the extent of our "yes", this mysterious exchange is also brought about for us and in us. We are taken up into the divinity of the One who took on our humanity. The Eucharist is the means, the instrument of this reciprocal transformation which always has God as its goal, and as the main actor. He is the Head and we are the limbs, he is the Vine and we the branches. Whoever eats of this Bread and lives in communion with Jesus, letting himself be transformed by him and in him, is saved from eternal death: naturally he dies like everyone and also shares in the mystery of Christ's Passion and crucifixion, but he is no longer a slave to death and will rise on the Last Day to enjoy the eternal celebration together with Mary and with all the saints.[178]

Let us place [...] our hand in Mary's maternal hand; may the Queen of All Saints lead us towards our heavenly homeland, in the company of the blessed spirits "from every nation, people and language" (cf. *Rv* 7:9).[179]

## Endnotes

[1] Cf. Lk 1:26-56; 2:5-7, 22-35, 41-52.
[2] Cf. *Catechism of the Catholic Church* 2709-2724, on "Contemplative Prayer"
[3] St John Paul II, Apostolic Letter on the most Holy Rosary, *Rosarium Virginis Mariae*, 16th October 2002 (RVM).
[4] Cf. RVM 3, 10, 11.
[5] RVM 3 (italics in original).
[6] RVM 11.
[7] RVM 12.
[8] RVM 1.
[9] RVM 19.
[10] Paul VI, Apostolic Exhortation on the right ordering and development of Devotion to the Blessed Virgin Mary, *Marialis Cultus*, 2nd February 1974 (MC), 46.
[11] MC 46.
[12] RVM 13.
[13] Cf. RVM 1, 3, 9, 18.
[14] Cf. RVM 15.
[15] Francis, Audience, 1st May 2013.
[16] Francis, Angelus, 6th October 2013.
[17] Pius XII, Letter to the Archbishop of Manila, *Philippinas Insulas* (1946); Paul VI, MC 42, 44; St John Paul II, RVM 1, 19.
[18] RVM 24.
[19] RVM 30 (italics in original).
[20] RVM 5.
[21] MC 46.
[22] RVM 26.
[23] St Josemaría Escrivá, *Holy Rosary*, Scepter, New York, 2002, p. 9: "To the Reader".
[24] Joseph Ratzinger-Benedict XVI, *Jesus of Nazareth*: *From the Baptism in the Jordan to the Transfiguration*, Bloomsbury, London, 2007, pp. 250-252.
[25] Benedict XVI, Homily at the Canonization of Frei Antonio de Sant'Ana Galvao O.F.M., Sao Paolo, Brazil, 11th May 2007.
[26] Cf. RVM 16, 39; Benedict XVI, Homily at the Pontifical Shrine of Pompeii, 19th October 2008.
[27] RVM 25.
[28] Francis, Homily at Castel Gandolfo, 15th August 2013.
[29] Francis, Angelus, 17th November 2013.
[30] Benedict XVI, Angelus, 1st October 2013.
[31] Francis, Words after Recitation of the Rosary at the end of the Marian month, 31st May 2013.
[32] Second Vatican Council, Dogmatic Constitution on the Church, *Lumen Gentium* 1: "The Church is in Christ like a sacrament or as a sign and instrument of a very closely knit union with God and of the unity of the whole human race".
[33] RVM 40 (italics in original).
[34] RVM 41 (italics in original).
[35] Cf. MC 52-54.
[36] Francis, Homily, 27th October 2013.
[37] Benedict XVI, Angelus, 1st October 2006.
[38] Homily [Santa Maria di Leuca, Italy] 14th June 2008.
[39] Angelus, 8th December 2006.
[40] Angelus, 17th December 2009.
[41] Angelus [Vienna], 9th September 2007.
[42] Homily, 15th August 2009.
[43] Regina Caeli, 31st May 2009.
[44] Angelus, 20th December 2009.

[45] Angelus, 25th September 2005.
[46] Homily [Parish of Our Lady of Consolation, Rome], 18th December 2005.
[47] Angelus, 23rd December 2007.
[48] Homily, 24th December 2007.
[49] Homily, 25th December 2005.
[50] Homily, 1st January 2008.
[51] Homily, 24th December 2007.
[52] Angelus, 4th January 2009.
[53] Audience, 27th December 2006.
[54] Homily [Mariazell, Austria], 8th September 2007.
[55] Homily, 25th December 2008.
[56] Angelus, 26th December 2006.
[57] Angelus, 26th December 2006.
[58] Homily, 31st December 2009.
[59] Angelus, 6th January 2009.
[60] Homily, 2nd February 2006.
[61] Homily, 2nd February 2011.
[62] Homily, 2nd February 2012.
[63] Homily, 2nd February 2006.
[64] Address, 2nd February 2009.
[65] Angelus [Brindisi, Italy], 15th June 2008.
[66] Angelus, 27th December 2009.
[67] Angelus, 31st December 2006.
[68] Angelus, 27th December 2009.
[69] Angelus, 31st December 2006.
[70] Homily, 13th January 2008.
[71] Angelus, 13th January 2008.
[72] Angelus, 11th January 2009.
[73] Homily, 7th April 2007.
[74] Angelus, 11th January 2009.
[75] Angelus, 13th January 2008.
[76] Homily [Pompeii], 19th October 2008.
[77] Homily [World Meeting of Families, Valencia, Spain], 9th July 2006.
[78] Homily, 8th December 2005.
[79] Homily [Altötting, Germany], 11th September 2006.
[80] Angelus, 21st September 2008.
[81] Angelus, 27th January 2008.
[82] Angelus, 14th October 2007.
[83] Angelus, 11th March 2007.
[84] Angelus, 25th March 2007.
[85] Homily, 29th September 2007.
[86] Angelus, 11th March 2007.
[87] Angelus, 9th December 2007.
[88] Angelus, 4th March 2007.
[89] Angelus, 8th March 2009.
[90] Angelus, 4th March 2007.
[91] Angelus 17th February 2008
[92] Angelus, 6th August 2006.
[93] Angelus, 17th February 2008.
[94] Angelus, 4th March 2007.
[95] Regina Caeli [Jerusalem], 12th May 2009.
[96] Homily, 5th April 2007.
[97] Angelus, 14th June 2009.
[98] Homily [via satellite for the Closing of the 49th International Eucharistic Congress, Quebec, Canada], 22nd June 2008.
[99] Angelus, 11th September 2005.
[100] Angelus, 25th May 2008.
[101] Angelus, 10th June 2007.
[102] Homily, 5th April 2007.
[103] Angelus, 11th September 2005.
[104] Angelus, 10th June 2007.
[105] Homily, 11th June 2009.
[106] Audience, 8th October 2008.
[107] Homily [Parish of the Holy Face of Jesus, Rome], 29th March 2009.
[108] Homily [San Giovanni Rotondo, Italy], 21st June 2009.
[109] Homily, 6th February 2008.
[110] Angelus, 31st August 2008.
[111] Angelus, 5th July 2009.

[112] Audience, 9th August 2006.
[113] Audience, 8th April 2009.
[114] Homily, 15th April 2007.
[115] Homily [Aosta, Italy], 24th July 2009.
[116] Angelus, 5th July 2009.
[117] Angelus, 26th November 2006.
[118] Angelus, 22nd November 2009.
[119] Angelus, 23rd September 2007.
[120] Angelus, 25th February 2007.
[121] Homily [Parish of the Holy Face of Jesus, Rome], 29th March 2009.
[122] Angelus, 26th December 2007.
[123] Homily [Parish of the Holy Face of Jesus, Rome], 29th March 2009.
[124] Audience, 15th April 2008.
[125] Angelus, 10th February 2008.
[126] Audience, 21st February 2007.
[127] Audience, 6th February 2008.
[128] Angelus, 13th September 2009.
[129] Audience, 5th November 2008.
[130] Angelus, 31st August 2008.
[131] Angelus, 17th September 2006.
[132] Homily, 25th November 2007.
[133] Audience, 29th October 2008.
[134] Homily, 24th December 2007.
[135] Homily, 28th June 2009.
[136] Audience, 12th April 2006.
[137] Angelus, 25th February 2007.
[138] Audience, 14th June 2006.
[139] Homily [Lourdes], 14th September 2008.
[140] Homily [Lourdes], 15th September 2008.
[141] Homily [Santa Maria di Leuca, Italy], 14th June 2008.
[142] Regina Caeli, 13th April 2009.
[143] Angelus, 2nd November 2008.
[144] Homily, 15th August 2008.
[145] Audience, 4th April 2007.
[146] Homily, 7th April 2007.
[147] Homily, 15th April 2006.
[148] Audience, 5th November 2008.
[149] Audience, 11th April 2007.
[150] Homily, 22nd March 2008.
[151] Homily [Vespers, Monte Casino], 24th May 2009.
[152] Homily [Mass, Monte Casino], 24th May 2009.
[153] Regina Caeli, 4th May 2008.
[154] Homily [Mass, Monte Casino], 24th May 2009.
[155] Regina Caeli, 8th May 2005.
[156] Regina Caeli, 20th May 2007.
[157] Homily [World Youth Day, Sydney], 20th July 2008.
[158] Homily, 31st May 2009
[159] Regina Caeli, 27th May 2007.
[160] Homily [Santa Maria di Leuca, Italy], 14th June 2008.
[161] Homily, 31st May 2009.
[162] Homily, 11th May 2008.
[163] Audience, 16th August 2006.
[164] Angelus, 15th August 2006.
[165] Angelus, 15th August 2009.
[166] Angelus, 15th August 2006.
[167] Angelus, 15th August 2009.
[168] Angelus, 15th August 2005.
[169] Homily, 15th August 2007.
[170] Homily, 15th August 2005.
[171] Homily, 15th August 2005.
[172] Angelus, 15th August 2008.
[173] Angelus, 23rd November 2008.
[174] Angelus, 26th November 2006.
[175] Angelus, 8th December 2008.
[176] Angelus, 26th November 2006.
[177] Homily, 15th August 2007.
[178] Angelus, 16th August 2009.
[179] Angelus, 1st November 2008.